I Heard a Train

poems by

Nancy Beauregard

Finishing Line Press
Georgetown, Kentucky

I Heard a Train

ACKNOWLEDGMENTS

Thank you to the following editors and publications in which these poems were previously published:

Contemporary Haibun Online: "Blindness"
SFCC Student Accolades: "Warty Toads" and "Bleached Bones"
Santa Fe Literary Review: "A Murder of Crows"

Publisher: Leah Maines
Editor: Christen Kincaid
Cover Art: Jeffery Cardin
Author Photo: Sabra LaVaun Romero, www.sabralavaunphotography.com
Cover Design: Elizabeth Maines McCleavy

Printed in the USA on acid-free paper.
Order online: www.finishinglinepress.com
also available on amazon.com

Author inquiries and mail orders:
Finishing Line Press
P. O. Box 1626
Georgetown, Kentucky 40324
U. S. A.

Table of Contents

To my daughter, Brittney,
and all my cheerleaders

Kool-Aid

funny, how you thought you were so grown-up,
smoking Kool cigarettes when you were twelve,
and drinking, drinking, drinking when you toured Vietnam,
learning to sleep drunk on the hard ground,
tough for your parents to see you passed out
on their front lawn

funny, how I thought you would stop when we married and
had kids, but they still made Kool cigarettes and you
were a man who drank blackberry brandy in bottomless
coffee cups filled with crushed ice

not so funny, how a body sounds when it falls unconscious down
the cellar stairs, the splintering of wood, the crash on cold cement,
the sticky sweet purple juice mixed with porcelain shards dripping
down the wall behind your head, while underneath your temple,
a red stain crept

I never could wash it out

Blindness

I watch the world recede through a telescopic lens. First the stars disappear, not one by one, but by constellations. Only the North Star remains, refusing to leave me. Up in the night sky it burns the brightest and my lips part in wonder. Colors that I thought once loved me have turned their backs and are now apathetic. The greens turn to gray, reds to orange, purples to blue. My field of vision no longer sees rivers winding through a meadow of lavender, or a desert of red cliffs. It is more specific, like looking at a hive of bees and seeing only one alight on a cactus blossom.

honey bees
yellow flowers
in shades of violet

Animal Crackers

Part I: All Aboard!

I heard a train.

I leaned against the white-washed fence,
watched you graze,   watched you chew,
          each delicate blade,
over and over again.

Jeweled coats of wavy brown,
backs twitched,   flies bit,
          tails swished,
while you do-si-doed.

I heard a train.

I shielded my eyes with my hand,
watched you plod   up that wooden ramp,
          into the darkened boxcar,
yellow numbered earrings jingled.

I climbed into the empty field,
pies steaming,   and for an instant,
          you stared at me,
from the slats of the moving metal car.

I heard a train.

I saw your big soft eyes,
under thick eyelashes,   scared and confused,
          pleading for release,
back into the fields still wet with tears.

I ran after you on shaky legs,
tripped on railroad ties,   screamed back at the engine's roar,
       my voice broken,
I would have named you Jacob.

Part II: The Circus Is In Town!

I heard a train.

In the middle of the night,
under a full moon,   stopped by a field,
       with a white-washed fence,
where cattle no longer danced.

I watched from my window,
the disguised wagons,   shadows in the dark,
       bars to keep you in,
Hell, they are bars to keep me out.

I heard a train.

You looked so cheerful,
on my cardboard box   of animal crackers,
       when I was five,
I ate elephants, tigers, and bears.

I didn't know about abuse,
bull hooks, whips,   shock prods and beatings,
       to make you entertain,
I didn't notice your chained feet or collars.

I heard a train.

Loud voices protesting your treatment,
woke me from a deep sleep,   many years ago,
                    my soul,
ashamed to have eaten those crackers.

No more animals in the circus,
the scars remain,   life not always,
                    considered a precious thing,
I stopped by a field with a white-washed fence.

Part III: I'll Blow Your House Down!

I heard a train.

Chugging up my driveway,
where no train should be,   gaining speed,
                    tearing up concrete,
you left debris on ghostly tracks.

I cowered in a corner of the basement,
water pouring,   from an earthen bowl,
                    around my feet,
you walked upstairs as if you owned the place.

I heard a train.

You ran through a tunnel,
in a deserted field,   by a white-washed fence,
                    a German shepherd,
clutched a thunder shirt in his mouth.

No birds in the sky,
under rocks,   over uprooted trees,
                    in a stream,
people stared at an upside-down house.

I heard a train.

When you left for the big city,
a mother covered her daughter,   with her own body,
                    in the bathtub,
she perished, protecting her child.

After the destruction,
I absently watched,   insects and bees,
              pollinate wildflowers,
perched on a dead sapling, a Whippoorwill calls.

Part IV: Unmarked Graves

I heard a train.

It matched the voice in my head,
the whisper on the tracks,   the conception,
                    in my womb,
life stirred in the fertile field.

I was joyously pregnant,
a little boy I was told,   with midnight hair,
                  stars for eyes,
at the end of my first trimester.

I heard a train.

When they delivered you,   after I miscarried,
                in a paper lunch bag,
not big enough to be buried in a coffin.

I dreamt of you the other day,
the years that followed,   playing with toys,
                    the train was so fast,
I never had the chance to name you.

I heard a train.

I stood in your small office,
the one with no windows,   no photos on the desk,
                    of your family,
and I wondered if you had one.

I noticed your accent and asked about your life,
you were born in Poland,   your beautiful wife,
                    killed in a gas chamber,
I heard the train whistle.

Part V: Up For Adoption!

I heard a train.

That boarded homeless children,
into boxcars made for people,   notes pinned to small jackets,
                    new families,
waiting for the Orphan Train at the depot.

Thousands paraded on stages,
singing ditties, reciting poems,   hoping for a mom and dad,
                    poked and prodded,
some to become farm hands, servants, or finally part of a family.

I heard a train.

I leaned against the white-washed fence,
watched you graze,   watched you chew,
            each delicate blade,
over and over again.

Jeweled coats of wavy brown,
backs twitched,   flies bit,
            tails swished,
while you do-si-doed.

I heard a train.

You had big soft eyes,
under thick eyelashes,   long spindly legs,
            a foal,
lost in a herd crying for its mother.

I ran after you on shaky legs,
tripped on railroad ties,   screamed back at the engine's roar,
            my voice broken,
I name you Jacob.

Warty Toads

A black entity zigzags across roads
People leave their cars and race for cover
While in a still puddle jump warty toads

Hail stings, wind whips, rain swells rivers
Roofs, cows, doors, a red couch floats, hovers
A black entity zigzags across roads

In a basement, my dog and I shiver
I call my daughter, and say I love her
While in a still puddle jump warty toads

A thirty foot pine stands straight, but quivers
Like a new bride waiting for her lover
A black entity zigzags across roads

Branches fly, propel themselves like slivers
Stuck in walls, through windows I discover
While in a still puddle jump warty toads

The town, a postcard cut with scissors
It will take years to recover
A black entity zigzags across roads
While in a still puddle jump warty toads

Murder on a Hot Summer Afternoon

The swing creaks, gliding forward and back while my
mother and I sit on its cushioned seats drinking cool tart
lemonade, and the wasps buzz above our heads in their
paper nest built against the jutting logs of my parents' home.

We watch my father, lost in his crazed power of gardening,
cutting the grass, trimming the plants, while sweat glistens
on his face, and drips down the front of his white t-shirt.

I swat and miss a flying gnat dive bombing my ice-filled glass,
I hear the buzz of honey bees flitting across a yellow pasture
and idly wonder why they have not made a nest behind us
instead of these angry stinging creatures.

We laugh talking about every day life as we watch my father's
slim, wiry hands come closer to my mother's small plum tree,
a sapling that he gave her on Mother's Day.

I worry that he will get carried away while pruning the branches,
but my mother is confident he will do the right thing,
we watch as he brings up the hedge clippers and
in one instance snaps the thin trunk in half.

Free
Falling

off the
Rio Grande
Gorge Bridge
like sky diving
into a cool Monet
pond aiming for a lily pad,
a small green dot
far below the horizon
you know you can do it,
wind whispers in my ear
while my heart beats
wildly in my chest
like the first time
we made love
or the last time
your heart stopped,
I pass mountains
on the way down,
unmoving, judging me,
I hear my mother's voice
telling me
we are born to die,
so quickly
the earth is coming up
to caress my face
or is it my father
who misses me
on the other side
where I am
so close to seeing him
I can smell his tobacco
sage, lavender
ready to cushion my landing
while fate has other plans
that pull me back
from the dream into reality
inches from hitting the ground.

Three Sisters

On the edge of a forest, so dark you cannot see the three tiny sisters hiding under the fallen leaves. Their noses are pink, their whiskers so sheer, their shaking tails curl around each other in fear.

See
the ransom note flutter just outside their cover. It calls them to discover the cure it holds within. As one they creep out listening for the slightest of sounds, trembling but brave, the three think of answers they crave.

How
can it be? They had stayed together so long, trying their best to stay strong. Cut letters, scratch and sniff, the aroma of aged cheese pulling them in. Hope still reads the words, but Despair feels their fate is sealed. Determined believes they will finally be healed.

They
know it's the farmer's wife, demanding they give her, well, everything: their sight, hearing, independence, and sanity, giving up every bit like a person's humanity. She says, "If you ever want to find the cure, there are handicaps you must first endure."

Run
the farm, the smell will guide them there. Bags of oats, barley, rice, their sharp teeth to gnash and tear. Fill their hungry bellies, comfort food to ease the pain, on this the day of their bloody campaign.

See
the kitchen so evil, shadows with eyeballs that cannot see, stolen and placed in jars, for pies, cakes, and sweet meats. The pot above the fire smells of roasting lamb and they wonder what they did for their souls to be damned.

How
do they escape the carving knife Mrs. Usher holds in her fist? "Look out!" they scream as it thrusts down to give Hope a kiss. She sidesteps smartly but Despair is too slow, and she loses her tail when she feels the blow.

They

turn to Determined who raises her own in defense, she wields it like a foil, the end puncturing the woman's shins. Hope joins in the fight lunging with all her might. She knows to kill the disease it must be cut off at the knees.

Run

skip, and jump, the farmer's wife is unable to continue the fight. The sisters have won the day, knowing that the cure is on the way. All they have to do is believe. They will not pay her ransom's price because they are not the three blind mice.

A Bay Leaf for Luck

The morning after you left

I could smell breakfast cooking in
the kitchen, like the ones you used
to make us kids, standing at the stove
in your flannel green and grey shirt,
spatula in hand, flipping pancakes,
the size of dinner plates.

Mismatched dishes on a plastic
polyester-backed tablecloth, silver-
ware we always made sure was clean,
fresh squeezed orange juice, bacon,
crisp and crumbly, dripping lard on
paper towels.

We fight—for the first butter
pancake, golden brown around
the edges, at least an inch thick,
maple syrup, sometimes store
bought, this time real.

The second morning after you left

On the plane to the east coast,
I could smell instant coffee, going
stale, the milk curdling, in your
stainless-steel thermos, some-
where over the Connecticut River.

Puckering your lips, taking a sip,
you stand in your torn v-neck
t-shirt, paint splattered work pants,
Santa Fe on your baseball cap,
covered in sawdust, from making
bird houses, bobbing flamingos,
and benches.

I unpack my suitcase, at my brother's
house, smell the pot roast, brown
potatoes, carrots, pearl onions, thick
gravy, bubbling on top the stove, I
know Mom is here, cooking, enticing
you to go, I haven't seen her in years.

The fourth morning after you left

I could smell spaghetti in the silent
moving car, red on a bed of white
noodles, meatballs, so thick and
round, browned in a skillet, then
toppled into the bubbling sauce.

Garlic, salt, pepper, a pinch of
sugar, I smell the fresh bread, their
crusty tops covered with blue and
white dish towels, cooling on metal
racks, set on an orange Formica
countertop, waiting to be sliced.

The secret ingredient, a bay leaf,
slides into the sauce, I wait to see
who the lucky person will be, to
get it on their spaghetti, Oh Please,
let it to be me, I pray, so I can
make the wish, that this is not the
day of your funeral.

Bleached Bones

A man proud of his kill,
the elk's bones bleached after
a few seasons in the woods.
There is no burial,
no words of gratitude,
for the meat in his freezer.
He passes the carcass on
his yearly hunt,
not seeing the beast's spirit
running free to
play among the trees.
His house is full of trophies,
racks with points,
leading to other worlds.
Thick skins where hearts
no longer beat,
on the floor
to warm his feet,
or drop crumbs on.
Mounted heads with pleading,
scared empty eyes,
he fondly remembers killing.
I sip my coffee in a room
full of people
and cringe inside
as he tells me
his hunting stories,
puffed up with pride
at slaying helpless beings.
I wonder as he is talking
what will happen when
he dies, what
will people say
when they pass
by his casket and
look at his bleached
bones.

A Murder of Crows

Opening the garage doors at 7am,
sunshine peeking through tall green pines,
maple leaves, orange, red, yellow,
and brown on the ground.

The smell of strong coffee,
a bite of cider doughnut,
the sugar crystals falling
on the cold hard driveway.

I pull out chairs, my grandfather's
toolbox, mom's pots and pans,
a haunted headboard, the ghost
comes with it free.

Mom's Cracker Barrel rocking chair,
a heavy cement deer on the front lawn,
missing its antlers from the tornado,
I wonder who has those.

I tighten my wool sweater,
seeing the crows, not in the trees,
but lined up in the road in
pickup trucks, cars, and SUVs.

They are waiting for the clock
with the golden hands to strike 8,
so they can flap their wings,
and descend on the house.

"How much is this dish, this book, these earrings?"
"I'll take $2 for that; No, I won't come down to $1.50."
The maple leaf table and chairs where we ate and played cards,
"SOLD" with the paintings on the walls.

Old linens in a steamer trunk, glass bowls, and antique dolls,
bird houses and bobbing flamingos my dad made,
their little pink heads with plastic eyes and straw hats,
I am keeping one of those.

At 5pm I am exhausted, my coffee is cold,
winter is coming, and the crows have flown home,
we pull in what's left to go to Goodwill,
the headboard goes in the trash, its ghost too.

Suitcases, boxes headed for Santa Fe,
filled with recipes, a photo of Dad on a horse,
one of the few pictures my mother painted,
and memories I would never sell.

Winter Warning

early morning—the sky a winter grey, the same
color as your faded police uniforms stored in
cardboard boxes on our basement shelves

boots crunch snow like potato chips—I breathe in the
crisp stillness, scrape car windows—while crow calls
above in the tree you planted years before your death

what is he warning—I wonder, getting in the car,
tightening my seatbelt, blasting heat, while the wind
lifts him to another snowy branch

I head down the mountain—hearing your voice
telling me to breathe—just breathe, while
my car fish-tails on black ice

Police Give Good Funerals

The First Gun Salute

My body jumps

running mascara, running children, the tear in my stocking running down, into the muted, muddy colors of a Persian rug beneath my sinking heels, I reach for a tissue box, I reach for a white gloved hand, resting across your light blue uniform with its tin badge,

a small heart of pink and white roses, a Winnie the Pooh bear from your daughter who knew you couldn't sleep without it, a solemn police guard, wreaths that read "To My Brother In Blue," a last kiss on cold lips, daring you to blink, to breathe just once before they close the lid.

The Second Gun Salute

My body jumps

feeling pain, the coldness seeping into living bones, in the church, the priest sprinkles holy water where nothing will grow, *Sobbing—* hearing your daughter play "Amazing Grace" on her violin, one last time for you,

men in uniforms, blue, grey, green, and brown, carry you past their cruisers, past the one with the black sash across the hood, the fire engines, the bus transporting officers and their dogs, all lined up for a final parade to the cemetery.

The Third Gun Salute

My body jumps

sitting on a metal chair, thinking about the baby you helped a mother save, the woman you stopped from being raped, thinking about our plans for the future, while Marines fold your flag and give it to your son, we listen to bag pipes in the distance, I place a rose on your casket, leaving you behind to rest, to sleep, to dream,

we walk to the cars for a farewell lunch of sawdust and bitter soda, cruiser 44 gives a last blast of the siren, I watch a police dog turn his head, not toward the sound but behind him, where you are, not in that box about to be buried, but instead on your way to answer the call.

Additional Acknowledgments

I also wish to thank:

Miriam Sagan, my poetry professor, who pushed me without pushing to go deep within myself and bring those emotions I was feeling to the surface.

My daughter, Brittney Beauregard, who read, edited, and encouraged me—I could not have done this without you.

Julia Deisler, Mekah Gordon, Louise Sedona, Serena Rodriguez, Ann Clemons, Judy Walker, Shuli Lamden, Daniel Zamora, Catherine LeBaigue, Kate McCahill, and Donald Anderson for your feedback, advice, and most of all your friendship.

My brother, Jeff Cardin, who searched and found the perfect train image for the cover of my book—and for believing in me.

Sabra LaVaun Romero for taking so many photos—and capturing the real me.

Mom, Dad, and Roger—who always had faith in me.

The publisher, editors, and staff at Finishing Line Press who made this chapbook possible.

Nancy Beauregard is a confessional poet who writes about the intense grief of losing the ones we love and the battles we fight to survive. She raised two children as a single mother after her husband's sudden death and has faced fear in a basement with a tornado raging above which left her New England town severely crippled. From writing about the hardships of living in a police family to the close-knit relationship with her parents, the poetry that results from her experiences is wracked with emotion and is able to connect with the reader on a deep level. After moving to New Mexico, she received the Richard Bradford Creative Writing Scholarship at Santa Fe Community College for her unique style of writing. On an even more personal note, Nancy battles Usher's disease, a condition that causes blindness and hearing loss, but she does not allow it to define her. She is presently an undergraduate student at the Institute of American Indian Arts studying poetry and fiction. She is writing her first murder mystery manuscript.